A REFLECTIC

A Reflection of God

Poems, Meditations, Prayer Resources

JOANNA TULLOCH

2014

Matador
9 Priory Business Park
Kibworth Beauchamp
Leicestershire LE8 0RX, UK
Tel: (+44) 116 279 2299
Fax: (+44) 116 279 2277
Email: books@troubador.co.uk
Web: www.troubador.co.uk/matador

ISBN 978 1784620 646

British Library Cataloguing in Publication Data.
A catalogue record for this book is available from the British Library.

Printed and bound in the UK by TJ International, Padstow, Cornwall

Matador is an imprint of Troubador Publishing Ltd

Acknowledgements

I would like to thank all those who have read and commented on my poetry over the years or encouraged me to publish it, including Marion Andrews, Sue Barratt, Anne Bartlett, the Revd Philip Beuzeval, Sue Beuzeval, Shirley du Boulay, Kaye Burton, Allie Butler, Freda Cammack, Robyn Claydon, Chris Cowley, Jo Dickinson, Fay Draper, Sister Elizabeth Jane CSJB, the Revd George Fryer, Mary Gilson, Dulcie Glassborow, Charlotte Graves Taylor, Maureen Grigg SHCJ, Gilli Hanna, Marlene Hickin, the Revd Jean King, Judith Lancaster SHCJ, Glenda Lane, Olive Leech, Ann Lewin, the late Mother Mary Jean SSC, David and Clare Matthews, Stephen Merson, Oona Mohan SHCJ, Joan Moore, the late Jack and Kathie Neary, Robert and Jennie Neary, the Revd Heather Noel Smith, Christopher Palmer, Annie Peel, Ann Persson, Jan Pollard, Linda Proud Smith, Derek and Lindsay Rawson, Grace Riddell, the late Wendy Robinson, Mary Ronaldson, David Scroggie, Neville and Beryl Shepherd, Julia Smith, Paul and Wendy Spray, Marcella Spreadbury, Azizë Stirling, the Revd Brian Tebbutt, Esther de Waal, Edmund and Clare Weiner, the Revd Bob Whorton, Allegra Wint, Constantina Wood, Julie Young, and others. Special thanks to the Rt. Revd Rowan Williams for his encouragement and commendation. I am grateful for the support and technical help of all the team at Matador. Last but not least, I want to thank my husband George Tulloch for helping and supporting me in a multitude of ways, and especially for design, typesetting, copy-editing, and proofreading.

Contents

II *We Want to See Jesus: Meditations on Scripture and Icons*

III *For the World: Praying and Sharing*

This book is dedicated to my dog Rebel
and to all who have shown me reflections of God

A Reflection of God

Like a dog with a favourite bone
you refuse to give me up,
even run to fetch me and show me off
to your most honoured guests.
Even though I am chewed round the edges
and have lost my savour,
I can never lose my Saviour
or seem to you dull and discardable.

Even though I am a Rebel,
by many of my actions
dishonouring your name,
and have often chosen to ignore your commands,
still you call me back
and throw the ball of life for me again.
You doggedly seek me out
in the thickets in which I trap myself
and wade in to rescue me
from the yellow bog, the silted pond.

And you have, like the best of gundogs,
a soft, a gentle mouth
so as to retrieve me without further bruising.
Truly there was never such a friend,
such a trusting or trustworthy companion
for all my days. Let us walk together
and explore the world.

I

Glimpses of Grace

Steps on my Journey

Via Positiva

Go forward into the day, my soul
and do not fear,
though the night-time be tormenting
or the morning mournful.
Go forward
with courage and conviction,
carrying your cross
and knowing that Christ has gone before you.
Go forward—
even a single step of faith
will take you further
than any amount of wandering
among worldly cares.
Go forward
though the earth seem to melt away
before you,
for as you place your feet there
the bridge will be built and buttressed
beneath you.
No ifs, no buts, no chasing after shadows—
simply go forward
to where the Master waits to greet you.

Psalm 63: 7

'Because you are my help, I sing in the shadow of your wings.'

'Sing,' said the psalmist,
'Sing in the shadow of his wings.'
So I opened my mouth
and out came a plaintive keening,
not so much a melody
as a frightened howl of pain.
And I knew that my song could never be good enough,
I knew that the darkness could only get deeper,
and I bared my back and tensed me for the punishment.

'Thank you,' he said,
'yours shall be a precious song,
born as it is from suffering and grief.
Thank you for your honesty,
for you have sung yourself.'

Instead of the whip
I felt only a whisper,
the stroking of a feather,
the shadow,
the shadow of his wings.

Candle

I lay there in silence,
in silence,
the only witness
to a guttering flame;
in silence,
in darkness,
the only witness
to an angel's wing.
Was it a shadow
that fluttered
on the ceiling?
Was it a shadow
or feathers
from another world?
I shall prefer
the silence,
the vision:
guttering, after all,
is far too dull.

The Invitation to the Garden

I had entered
the jungle of the soul.
And it was a real jungle,
dark, wet, hot,
and swampy.
I was really there,
finally transported
to the slippery
rotting
claustrophobic
pit where I belong.
Many times
this swamp
had sucked me down,
but now
trapped in the yellow muck,
dripping yet thirsty,
hopeless and dirty,
I knew the nightmare
for what it was—
my life.

When I saw
the vision,
the hand of grace
extending through the trees,
I knew at once
that this must be
the Gardener,
I knew that he alone
could hear my cries.
It was just a hand really,
but never before
and never since
has such a hand been seen:

coming from light
it pointed to light,
transparent, yet
having substance,
real help
and real hope
to offer.
In the moment
of that courteous invitation
to step into the garden
from the mire,
in that turquoise and yellow moment
there was time and no time,
now and all time.
And oh
there was mercy,
and grace to believe in mercy,
grace to be accepted
and be loved.
Can I recreate
the silence?
It was
speaking
but no words,
music
but no tune,
silence fit to heal a thousand wounds.
And it was invitation:
'Come,
this is all for you,
please be my guest.
Without you
there cannot be a garden.
Come, if you will—
but only if you will—
to make my garden complete.'

Enough

'It is enough to want to want to love God.'
St Teresa of Avila

ENOUGH, she said, ENOUGH.
Wanting to want's enough.
And the floodgates wept
with all their holding
of the wanting to want,
and the soul's sigh
wafted the angels
with rivers of relief.

ENOUGH, one word, ENOUGH.
Wanting to want's enough.
And it shook this life
that had been spent in
always wanting to want,
scattering pale dust
into the cupboard
where hopes of joy had lain.

ENOUGH, you said, ENOUGH.
Wanting to want's enough.
And I took this dust
that some would scoff at,
knowing that you would not,
for a sure sign
that in the darkness
mercy still will grow.

Healing Service

White-water rafting
wasn't what I thought fun.
Urged, urged and carried
this way, that way
over rocks and stones,
shaken,
shaken not stirred
till every bone is broken,
every sense is gone.
O Holy Spirit,
you see my white knuckles,
know I am afraid,
shake me all over
(shaken *and* stirred).
My white scar tissue
under your dear hand shaking,
yet still you flow over me,
toss me on the rapids,
throw me to the ground.
Irresistible flow,
turbulent white river,
if I can ride your awesome raft
shall I at last find fun?

Coincidence?

Beyond the curtain, though I cannot see them,
there are separate wonders:
trees, and mist, and early-morning sun,
the countryside peacefully emerging,
pleased with a new day's clothing.
There are trees, and mist, and early-morning sun
singularly there, to be seen.
But there is just one brief moment
when all of these together
meet in a light embrace.
Is it coincidence I lift the curtain then?

February Flowers

The daffodils are hoping for an early spring,
racing the forsythia for flowering.
Feet still in frost, they feel the air
as if divining how to start behaving.

Some will be blind and never see the sun,
others will die before their flowers can open.
Still, they'll have tried. Crocus and snowdrop
cannot now claim all the early glory.

Colour me yellow in this coldest month,
sun-dipped and wind-whipped into a new daring.
Dapple me daffodil in my dreams and plans
so that the darkness shall not sap my courage.

Before the month is out I shall be rising
up, up to the life you'd have me living.

The Leaf

Is this the leaf that hid in the frosted twig,
silent but certain little bud of hope?

Is this the leaf that thrilled me in the spring,
clean green injection to my heart?

Is this the leaf the sun shot through with life
and, laughing, fell all dappled from the sky?

Is this the leaf that, even as it dies,
becoming dust, bleeds beauty from its pores?

YES, this one leaf is all I need to know
that God is great, and all my year is joy.

Flexible Stability

Supple I am not
nor much accustomed
to sitting on the floor
or on a prayer stool,
so meditation challenges
my body.
To be quiet and still
and let the thought-stream
flow like a breeze,
be noticed for what it is
then left to blow away,
never disturbing
the real sense below.
The golden tree I watch
in other moments,
its top level with my window,
shows me how it's done:
sprays of yellow green
constantly bobbing
and the twig-ends flexing
so that each puff of breeze
frills the leaves and
moves the branchlets,
waving and turning
them backwards,
but, as the gust releases,
lets them return alert,
while the roots
remain rock-solid
and the trunk's
a supple core,
merely bending gently
at its base.

Grey-Green

We met in the abbey cloister
among the slow, cool shadows
and gazed at pools of light.
The stones looked down grey-greenly.

I tried to speak my failure,
my poverty of loving,
the thinness of my friendship
and the courage I have lacked.

And then we both fell silent
while the stones looked down grey-greenly,
raising their algal eyebrows
at the story I had told.

I didn't hear you speaking
but the light-pools grew before us
and the stones looked down grey-greenly
with benevolence and peace.

And then I knew your message:
'If you cannot find the courage
and your love goes cold within you,
do not worry—just take mine.'

Thin Place: the Bushy Combe, Glastonbury

Come, take my hand
and climb the dewy hill,
drinking the grasses' mystery,
up to the womb hollow.
The combe follow,
the bushy broom's yellow.
Up, up above the mists
and the roots of love and birth
lies this dip,
this lip,
this open mouth
where you may lie
in the silent word of God,
stroked by his gracious touch
yet still, so still.
And when you are ready—
not yet—
when you are really ready
pluck a single tongue of grass,
fragile, yet strong,
to take upon your journey
in remembrance
of the growth you have known here.

Inner Landscape

Transported from the chapel where I sit
into something full and upright,
like looking down
from a tall tree in the forest.
The crown, I think they call it.
And there *is* here a dream of royalty,
a glimpse of glory,
and how it feels to sit upon a throne.
Or rather to *be* majestic,
to stand firm and untroubled,
full-favoured, buttressed,
like a mighty oak.
Or even taller and more regal,
Scots pine reaching for the sky.
From this vantage point
I see the forest,
its juices running
into age-old amber.
And I know my strength,
I know my beauty.

Feeble Frame

Well you know it, Lord,
how it has failed to carry
weight, or to model beauty,
how it has given way
under the load you had
foremeasured for it,
how it is tattered
with the rubbish it has hauled
(contraband from others
with no scales, no weighbridge),
labelled 'wanted on journey'.

Well you know, and yet
you are minded to forgive,
to pick me up parentally
and bear me gently
away from those false friends
whose only object
is to make me want things
and to weigh me down
with their cuckoo-in-the-nest desires
until the frame breaks
once again, feeble indeed.

I tend to snap,
but you just tend;
I go spare,
but you always spare me.
And so this feeble frame
of mind, spirit, body
that you know so well
and flood with wide-flowing mercy
bows before you,
and my soul
is filled with praise.

Déjà Vu

Strengthen the feeble knees, you said,
as we came upon this landscape once again.
You knew that mine were shaking, then,
the moment that the recognition dawned . . .
if night knocking, nauseously known,
can call itself aurora. Anyway,
you made me stand and look at the abyss
from which I'd crawled so drained those other times
and see it from above. And then
you offered me the brush, to paint
the blacks out silver and the mire to gold,
the grief leaf-yellow with a turquoise tint
and comfort in the shades. Okay,
I thought I had gone back, but see
it is not I now, it is we,
and, yoked, we're on our way.

Oratorio

The most exciting moment of the day—
sitting
sitting with a blank page before me
holding
holding a pencil in my hand
waiting
waiting to see what will be given
opening
opening my heart to receive
giving
giving my will over to the Other
silence
silence that lets the waters settle
reflecting
reflecting both our faces as on glass
changing
changing the tenor of the morning
into what?
The soprano of the day.

Still Small Voice

First there must be
the prayer
and only then
the poem—
it doesn't work
the other way around.
But it happens quietly.
I might think nothing
has been going on
but the singing silence
in my head,
nothing firing the synapses
between my ears,
and certainly
no eureka moment,
no communication
of 'the answer',
when suddenly
words begin to pour
on to the page
faster than I can
write them down,
like a dictation almost,
and I the secretary
needing so many per minute
for proficiency, and then
—just as suddenly—
they stop.

Sometimes the poem
is complete then,
but other times
I can feel it
still shaking down inside
until I give the bottle

a sharp tap
and the last drop
plops into place.
And it isn't
in the wind,
though there be
a proper storm inside,
and it isn't
in the earthquake,
though I be
shaken to the core,
and it isn't
in the fire either
that God speaks.
It's the soft scratching
of pencil on paper,
the silence of writing
and reading back,
the tumble of words
out of empty-headedness:
that is the still small voice
whose eloquence always
takes me by surprise.

Prayer Box

Across from me the prayer box hangs,
its coral cross invisible through reading glasses,
but even if I cannot see it, it is there.
Can I believe the same about the prayer?
Half an hour of breathing didn't do it,
nor did twenty rounds of Maranatha,
but by now I should not be expecting
anything but what comes free, unguided.
There is nothing in the prayer box hanging
with its coral cross that I cannot see,
but that doesn't mean that prayer is empty.
Presence or absence, silence or a rush of words,
images or just the miracle of breathing—
even when that marvel seems banal—
whatever is given or not given in the moment
must be cherished as the lesson for the day,
accepted and allowed to vanish on the out-breath.
Don't try to keep it in a box, for manna rots—
just celebrate its nourishment, or fasting.

By Beckley Mast

Have you withdrawn the gift
or have I lost the frequency—
not just the daily practice
but the spiritual tuning to receive it?
This I ask myself as much as you.
Looking for blocked arteries,
channels once open that no longer flow,
I remember how the poems
were my lifeblood, and their pulse
the power that pushed me forward,
the rhythm of my spirit
not so long ago.
I remember how words came
faster than I could write them,
urgent and undeniable,
arriving ready-formed on each day's page
and nothing was deleted,
no crossings-out or second thoughts,
no censorship of the morning's
broadcast to my soul.
So where is the interference
coming from? So different now
the jamming of the airwaves
and the laboured language,
the languishing over a word or phrase
only to delete it later angrily.

I can't think you've stopped broadcasting,
only that I have somehow missed your signal.
And so I search the short waves for your music,
knowing I cannot live far from your song.

Flagging

My prayers are just torn tatters
fluttering on a stony outcrop
changing direction with the wind
and barely anchored to the bluff.

Between a rock and a hard place
I stuff these poor petitions
hardly expecting an acknowledgement
let alone any meaningful reply.

And yet I have to hope
these forlorn flags flapping from the crevices
will anyway attract attention
for God is so much closer than we imagine

and always ready to receive our SOS.

Seven Years On: a Psalm

O Lord, hear my prayer, for I am lonely and afraid.
When I was tossed on the torrents of chaos
you were beside me, though I could not know it.
Do not let them pull me back in,
you who have heard me and raised me.
The waters came over my head, and I had drowned
but your power carried me high on to the beach.
The serpents of the deep still seek to devour me,
the ebb tide draws me back into their jaws.
Why have you wrung the water from my lungs
if bilge is to submerge me anyway?
No, I will hope in your cycle of seven—
the next big wave might push me up the shore.

A Way

I chant the mantras
you have given me before
of courage and of peace,
forgiveness and compassion.
I put my best foot
forward to the day,
remembering the *via positiva.*
Now I see the purpose
of the gift,
how it can sustain
through further trouble.
Be the firm ground
that I thought was gone,
be the promise
of a greater wholeness.
And let me know
a glimpse can be enough
to hold on to the vision
now emerging.

T-ing the C: Meditation Medication

Could this waiting space
this breath
be my turning point
of being
moment entered and remained in
shimmering silence
out of which the whisper
intimates allrightness?

Not a pill to be
swallowed
but the oxygen
of energy
air taken in deeply
then the shudder
as the answering release
expels all tension.

In this resting place
this heartbeat
is the beginning
of renewal
journey only just embarked on
inner landscape
starting to reveal itself
as longed-for wholeness.

Courage

Maybe I have scared
myself enough—
there is a point
beyond terror
where nothing can shake
you any more.
There is a point
deep in the eye
of the outrage
where punishment and pain
shrivel on the funeral pyre
of peace.
If I can learn to sit
just sit
with this shaming
darkness
I will come
to be so brave
that even love and mercy
are received—
compassion for myself
shall be
my firm, sure path
back home.

*'And you learn that you really can endure . . .'**

Funnily enough
I heard these words before I saw them.
They were spoken inside me
as a handsel of my soul.
I had just dared to open
the wallet of my blessings
to pour out all the coinage
in a fountain on the floor
and to realize that endurance
comes with the territory—
the power to bear your life
is suffering's reward.
And in your weakness is your strength.
It is like the soft scar tissue
silvery and fragile
thinner than your other skin
but flexible and strong.
The scabs will fall away
and I will ban them from my memory
so that the face all see
shall regard the world with love.

* This line, which has been variously but inconclusively attributed to a number of poets, may go back to a Spanish original in a poem by Jorge Luis Borges.

Psalm 63: 7 Revisited

All this time my guilt
has been unquestioned;
all these years I've thought
I was to blame.
That you forgave
and loved me anyway—
yes, that was a revelation.
You stroked me with the feather
as I waited for the whip.
But now in the silence
I hear another question:
for what am I *really* responsible?
Now I must answer
to the me that is becoming—
no false guilt or ugliness or shame.
That you find me blameless
and even beautiful
draws me from the shadows,
helps me grasp the real.
In your shelter
you have grown me new white feathers;
my turn now to test them,
caress with them,
risk flight.
It will not be easy
to leave self-blame behind me,
but yes, I will be-coming.
And, as I come, I sing.

Somewhere

Somewhere between four and seven
out of the tossing heat
and the squirming of anxiety,
out of the can'ts and won'ts—
words my mother taught me
have no claim to exist anyway—
somewhere, as the sun
surrounded the sycamore
and a pigeon on the roof
dropped gently on to the waiting air,
trusting it to carry the weight—
somewhere there
hidden in a moment I had thought
unbearable, slick and sticky
with the cloying sweat of fear—
somewhere I found the peace,
the piece of heaven hidden
as Fra Angelico said I would,
and, before it too could fly away,
I grasped it.

Soul Flight

It was a true communion,
an inner harmony,
buzzing with the throbbing gift of
energy. That raw place,
that bleeding hole in my spirit,
exquisitely painful
always up to now—suddenly
it felt filled, brimming up.
The taut-to-strangling strings wound down,
the note now sweet again,
and the bow was rosinous and
resonant, not choking.
Oh, I wish you could have heard it,
my own lark ascending,
and seen her flying off into the
misty morn, sure again.
No longer will there be a need
to crank up the engine
grindingly and with much groaning,
for there will be wing-tips
that whisper words of joy
to my inmost being.

I Am a Seagull

When I prayed, Jesus, I was like a broken bird
I'd seen you hold so tenderly and weep for.
Like a spaniel, with soft mouth, you picked me up
and carried me towards your master,
as someone said, 'Monica, we've got another one here!'
and white-robed women gathered round.
The salt in your tears stung in the wounds no-one had
touched
but I knew they would be like ointment, healing.
I knew I would learn to swim on their bobbing sea
and rise again above the waters,
wheeling, crying, gliding out upon the thermals,
for you had touched me inwardly, and I was free.

Eventually

You do not pursue
even when I try to hide
in the very deepest dodge-holes.
Rather you wait patiently
knowing I must come back out
eventually.

You do not condemn
even when I blame myself
or listen to my inner critic.
Rather you wait patiently
knowing I must feel your grace
eventually.

You do not command
even when I face a choice
to follow you or have my way.
Rather you wait patiently
knowing I must hear your call
eventually.

You do not give up
even when I fail to turn
to you for everything I need.
Rather you wait patiently
knowing I must learn to pray
eventually.

II

We Want to See Jesus

Meditations on Scripture and Icons

The Garden

While living in the middle of the jungle,
is there not a garden we all seek,
vaguely remembered, or maybe only dreamed of:
do we not long to have it in our sight?

Can we not hear its music in our silence,
a great sad song of longing, yet of joy,
the song sung by a gentle, lonely Gardener:
do we dare to listen, touch the tree of life?

They heard the sound of the Lord God walking in the garden in the heat of the day . . . And God said to Eve, 'What is this that you have done? . . . I will increase your labour and your groaning.' And he put them out of the garden.

And Jesus said to Mary Magdala, 'Why are you weeping? Who is it that you seek?' And, thinking that he was the gardener, she said, 'Tell me where you have taken him.' And Jesus said, 'Mary.' One word. And then she knew.

The song once heard can never be forgotten,
it is the restless music of our souls;
but never say our free will has been forfeit:
we choose, all right, whether to weep or dance.

Creation and fall, resurrection and re-creation. See Genesis 3 and John 20.

Rood Tree

Following a light shower
the sky has brightened
and the wet ivy scintillates,
winking in the breeze.
There is a whole world
in that familiar sycamore,
a community of doves and pigeons,
a playfulness of squirrels,
and many other lifeforms
that I cannot see from here.
But the ivy is slowly strangling the tree,
wrapping its trunk and branches
in a green-white-yellow ligature,
squeezing it to death like a boa constrictor
while pretending—and managing—
to look so fine.
If the tree falls it will flatten our house,
but it stands in another garden
so there's nothing we can do
to stop the serpent hissing and threatening.
We cannot cut the ivy at its roots;
all we can do is listen
to the creaking in the wind, and worry.
Once in another garden a woman listened
to a serpent, and was led astray, away from God.
Was that the moment when anxiety began?
Was it because people fell for forbidden fruit
and still sacrifice all for it?
Was that when lies and blandishments
began their seduction
and love was cheapened to a browning apple core?
Sadly it was.
But here now stands a barer, starker tree
on which there hangs not ivy, but the body

of the living God, the dying God,
raising love again to the highest value,
bearing fruit that all of us may eat.
This tree will not fall
though we pile all our sin upon it;
this fruit will not fade
though we bite great chunks from it.
This love will not fail us
whatever we do to it—
for this Holy Rood ends all our fears,
antidote to anxiety.

The Cross: tree of knowledge, tree of life. See Genesis 3, Matthew 27: 35, Mark 15: 24, Luke 23: 33, John 19: 18.

Watershed

A silver ribbon rippling
between this high path
and the land beyond—
the unknown land of milk and honey
(or maybe of jam tomorrow)
its sweetness just a promise yet,
tickling the tastebuds into appetite.
'Choose life,' said Moses,
knowing that he would never cross
into that promise,
knowing the silver ribbon marked
the last page of his story here
but also the beginning of history,
of a new meandering river
leading him home and his people on
into such a saga as the minstrels never sang
before or since. This ribbon
marks a parting of the ways,
the valley waiting there below
both final and strangely fertile,
leading to death and life.
I know which way I choose.

Moses dies before reaching the Promised Land.
See Deuteronomy 34.

Make a Straight Path

Lopsided Saviour
watching me from the bookshelf,
I didn't get your face quite right
and you have one ear, one eye, one eyebrow
higher than the other.
You have the unequal gaze also—
but that was deliberate—
one eye piercing and challenging,
the other sad and oozing compassion.
Even your halo isn't perfectly round,
and your beard, cheeks, and chin
are not equally balanced.
Yet you speak to me through all this imperfection
of what it means to say that God became human—
for I have never seen a human face
that was perfectly symmetrical
and, on another level,
every human being is flawed.
You tell me, yes, that I am far from perfect,
but when you look at me like that
with love and sorrow in your eyes
I know I only have to be good enough.
And your lips, which I nearly forgot to mention,
moved once to speak a single word to me—
LOVE: yours perfect, mine just the best that I can manage.
With that one word you said, 'Enough.
Receive my perfect love and do what you can with it
in the lopsided world.
Start with yourself and let it heal you
of all that is bent and broken in your life;
then, just be good enough
and my love will redress the balance.'
Lopsided Saviour,

I hear you. I see you.
You alone can straighten the crooked path.

Contemplating my first attempt to paint an icon of the face of Christ. Cf. Isaiah 40: 3, John 1: 23.

Archangel in Red and Yellow

Michael, Michael,
Captain of Israel's host, usually warlike
as you hunt the rebels down—
in this particular icon you are gentle,
supplicating on our behalf
as you stand there in the Deesis,*
beseeching Christ in glory
to send a few splinters of light
in our direction.
You need a coat of lacquer
for you are already a bit battered
from being carried round
and I see I shall have to repair you
before I make you glossy.
Or maybe not—
fighting evil as you do is a bruising business
and perhaps your battle-scars
should remain for all to see.
Michael, Michael,
holding your fine-boned hands out in supplication,
with strange teardrops birthing new feathers
on your corrugated wings,
intercede for us whose hands are rough and dirty
from living in the bruising world
and whose tears do not beget wings to fly on,
so that the perfect love
of the Lamb gracing the throne
might bathe us in red and yellow—
the red of his blood, the yellow of his glory—
so that we might become the icons
of God's humanity

* Deesis: the tallest row of an iconostasis, above the Royal Doors, in which Christ sits enthroned in the centre, and Mary, John the Baptist, Archangels, and Apostles stand on each side and intercede for us.

and be raised up above all base desires,
battered, but not defeated by the world,
and wringing, ringing
all the life and glory
that Christ squeezed out for us
from our most unpromising beginnings
to his most triumphant end.

An icon of the Archangel Michael (one of the first I attempted to paint). See Daniel 10: 13 & 21 and 12: 1, Jude 9, Revelation 12: 7.

The Archangel Raphael

Tobit was blind
and Anna wept fearful tears
convinced her son Tobias would be lost.
Sara saw seven husbands die on their wedding night
so she, too, was no stranger to pain and grief.
But into their story
stepped the young Azarias—
in truth the Archangel Raphael in disguise—
and showed Tobias how to use
the fish to banish tears,
its organs freeing Sara to marry him,
its gall giving sight to Tobit,
gall washing gall away.

For us the fish is the sign of Christ
and the gall the sacrifice of crucifixion.
Gall has washed gall away for ever now,
love has proved its power over death.
Wherever there are tears, wherever demons,
wherever there is blindness to the light,
there is also deep compassion hovering,
God's angels waiting in the wings
to perform the miracle again.
So if you feel like crying,
look on this gentle angel
who brought healing to a family
and know there is no gall
so bitter that God has not already rinsed it,
no family so broken
that Christ our brother cannot mend with love.

A lesson from the Apocrypha. See Tobit.

MiniMum

At the very least
you enabled the greatest miracle to happen.
Your 'let it be'
started the biggest story of all time,
allowing the Almighty
to become so tiny and so vulnerable,
a refugee, a nobody
caught up in the counting of all souls.
See him now,
his little face pinched and minimally painted,
looking up
into the fuller features of your face.
See him too
in every hungry, thirsty orphan,
in the pinched faces
of the very lowest of the low.
Can this be God?
Would God really choose so small a portion,
not just to be born
but to die that shameful, demeaning death?
Incredible but true—
that small pinched face is the image of the greatest
coming to save us
as if it were the least that God could do.

The Annunciation (contemplating a miniature icon of the Virgin and Child). See esp. Luke 1: 38.

*Mother of God of the Deesis**

Such deep sadness
falls from your eyes,
and yet it is a sadness
tempered by tenderness,
born of the gentlest stroking of a dry brush
against your cheeks,
softening the shadows
and framing your face
in a dark but human flesh.
The surprise of this gradual emergence
is something I will not forget, ever,
for as your face appeared,
so slowly and last of all
apart from the fine decoration,
to the tune of the teacher's 'little by little',
the awareness of your compassion
also grew within me,
swelling and fleshing out the face
of intercession.
Mary the Mother of God
hardly features in my Methodist tradition,
and yet I knew then for sure
that you *do* intercede for us,
Mother of Sorrows,
bearer of such deep pain.
In the Deesis you stand
beside Christ in glory
and everything about you—
eyes, lips, even the set of your shoulders—
speaks of compassion,
Christ's compassion for the world
nailed to the cross

* See p. 45.

and piercing your heart for ever.
Had you not stood there first
you wouldn't be here now in the Deesis—
for how could you intercede for us
without first suffering such grief?
Sad, tender mother
whose pain has made our joy complete,
you give the Deesis its depth.

Incarnation and Passion (contemplating an icon of Mary, the first that I was taught to paint by a Russian icon master). Cf. Luke 2: 35.

Mother of God of Perpetual Help

Help perpetual they call you
as you cradle the eternal child
in perpetuity,
one hand curved to support his body
like the bentwood rocker of a favourite chair,
the other holding the tiny hand
of all humanity,
the cheeks aligned in touching tenderness.
In your eyes, gazing unusually
straight into ours
is the deep understanding
of what it means to be a mother—
the love, the fear, the hurt, the pain, the joy
that cuts all mothers into tiny pieces
and yet also makes us whole—
and to know that you have made this journey
with sorrow and excitement
balanced in your hands
is to be helped, yes, always to be helped.
In later years,
after the trauma of the cross
and the turning upside-down of everything
that came with the resurrection,
once you were alone again,
how did you find your purpose?
Who could you be once you had been God's mother?
Didn't the child give you help perpetual
to be fully yourself,
whole and perfected even in the imperfection
he came to share, and live and die for?
And wholeness is the perpetual help
he offers us as well,

our cheeks touching tenderly
as we rock in that favourite chair.

Incarnation and Passion (contemplating an icon of the Virgin and Child). Cf. Luke 2: 35.

Mother of God of Yaroslavl

Holy Mother of God,
can you feel the caress your child is giving you,
stroking your chin
and cupping it in his hand?
You are called tenderness and compassion,
Eleousa, Mother of Mercy,
and it is true you cradle him
with a soft and gentle touch.
But first the love is flowing into you,
the love that the Lord chose to share
with the cold, cruel world
and nurtured in your womb,
chosen one of many.
For he is Immanuel, God-with-us.
and, though you still hold him there, a baby,
it will not be long now
before your heart is pierced
and we see,
we all see if we care to look,
that tenderness and compassion
flow through him
more tragically, more powerfully
as he cups in his hands
not your chin, not your robe,
but the hard iron nails of human hatred,
yet renders them in his dying moments
as soft as a baby's skin,
as tender as a mother's heart.

Incarnation and Passion (contemplating another icon of the Virgin and Child). Cf. Luke 2: 35.

Bread of Life

Soup as thick as stymied thought
in the dish of disconnected memory,
sticky and unswallowable
without a loaf to soak it up.
Ah, here comes nourishment,
here is the promised bread—
great thick doorsteps of puckly brown
or soft smooth rolls of white.
Broken for you this staple food,
for you these crumbs let fall—
remember this whenever you partake of it,
whether with pea soup in the brain
or wine at the communion table,
a simple meal with friends
or high in the sky from an airline meal-tray.
Ubiquitous and basic, yet so varied,
ready to meet every hungry human need,
bread, like Christ, is with you always,
Christ, like bread, is the staple of your life.
And all for you, every crumb for you is given
so that even sticky soup
will not burn your tongue and throat
but slip down easily
to nourish and restore.
For Jesus said, 'I am the bread of life'
and God is always baking white and brown,
heaven's ovens bursting with risen loaves
for every person brown or white in God's creation—
for you, for you, for you,
and, yes, for you.

Jesus feeds the multitude. See John 6, esp. 35 & 48.

Mindfulness

Here is bread, you said,
for the breaking and the taking,
once soft dough so pliable
under human kneading—
then the baking, and the making
of five small loaves so friable
their crumbs were five thousand's feeding.
For the taking and the breaking,
you said, here is bread.

I am the bread, you said,
for the living and the dying,
my risen life reliable
to end all human needing—
all sighing and all crying,
my cross identifiable
wherever love is leading
you to service, where you're trying
to share me. I am the bread.

Eat this bread, you said,
and remember our last sharing
here, before I drank the cup
of bitterness, and died for you—
how you were all despairing.
But remember how God raised me up
to the new life I have won for you,
and the banquet I'm preparing.
Mind, as you eat this bread.

Jesus feeds the multitude and shares the Last Supper with his friends. See esp. John 6 & 13.

Doom and Treacle

What did you dream of
as the boat was tossed
like a matchstick
on the boiling surf,
down into deep dark chasms
spilling over suddenly
into lightning,
and the crash following behind,
splintering the air
doom boom?

How did you manage
to stay asleep
through your friends' screams,
not rocked so much as
nose-dived and G-forced down and up,
slammed back against the stern
with super-whiplash
before they came to shake you,
wake you feebly
in their fear?

What foreknowledge held you
in its calm embrace
as things fell apart
around you,
and people too
were in pieces,
frantic before an unknown fate
but one they feared
they could forecast
all too clearly?

And then when they woke you
how did you command—
simply by holding up your hand—

all of the forces of creation?
Who are you that the wind
and waves obey you?
Whoever, whatever, wake with me
I beg you, and tell the
doom boom treacle that assails me
'Peace, be still.'

Jesus calms the storm. See Matthew 8: 23–7, Mark 4: 35–41, Luke 8: 22–5.

Soul Space

So where is the spirit
if not in the body
and where can the soul stir
free from the devious mind?
Every time the monologue
of thoughts breaks
the surface of the water
and my breathing becomes
laboured and self-conscious,
I have to take a step back
from the silent pool.
What I await
is a different disturbance—
the stirring of the water
by a healing hand.
This is the signal to approach,
to slip through the meniscus
and let the current take
me where it will.
If I can learn to trust
this stream of no-thought,
this floating free of selfishness,
there will be a wholeness
both within me and around me—
the uniting spirit's silver sea
where everyone may swim.

Jesus heals at the Sheep Pool. See John 5: 1–9.

Trees Walking

God Almighty,
are you?
Human all-suffering,
yes, you are certainly that.
Healer extraordinary,
making your medicine
out of mud,
out of the very dust
we are formed from.
At its first anointing
we can only see trees walking.
But if we let you
rub us with our own dirt again,
then there is real vision.
Teacher by example,
your lessons
make us not cleverer
but, if we can bear them,
humbler and wiser.
And even to see trees walking
is one step
towards moving a mountain.
Who made that man blind, they asked,
was it the fault of the parents?
No, no, you made it clear
it was not.
Rub dirt into my eyes, then, twice
and give me vision.
Give me wisdom
and, above all, humility.
Let me see the trees walking
and go on to believe
that yes, you *are* God Almighty,

maker and mover of mountains.
And whisper this message
to the grieving parent, too:
there is nothing,
nothing at all
with which to reproach yourself.

Jesus heals a man born blind. See Mark 8: 24, John 9.

What Am I?

What am I but a dirty mark,
a smudge marring the visage
of the Infinite?
Yet gazing on the Holy Face
find there a beauty spot that
is imprinted
over all this grubbiness—
cloth Christ not made with hands
wiping me clean.

What am I but the nickel dull,
base metal where the mirror's
lost its silvering?
Yet basking in the sun, the Son
who shines out to all compass points
with righteousness,
am rendered all reflective once again—
Christ the refiner's fire
restores my sheen.

What am I but a wayward child
distracted by the false allures
of worldliness?
Yet coming to myself I see
a loving parent holding out his arms to me,
mercy and grace embracing
my unworthiness
and never even asking
where I've been.

You greet me as your honoured guest
and say, as you invite me to the feast
to celebrate,
'However many times you run away

I'll always take you back with open arms.'
No more, then, is the question
'*What* am *I*?'
but *who*, by grace, *each* child of God
may be.

The Prodigal Son (partly inspired by icons of the Holy face and Immanuel). See Luke 15: 11–32.

Transfiguration

Was it a dream, or am I still asleep?
The whisper of a still, small voice
more like to waken me
than thunder.
The bearer of our people's Law
more like to lead me now
in wonder.
I am not sure
what I can see or hear,
but know my Master
changed,
translumined,
joined in light
with all the years,
our misunderstanding and fears,
the wandering and seeking,
as I observe him speaking
a word,
the word,
the only Word we need.

A mountain-top experience. See Matthew 17: 1–13, Mark 9: 2–13, Luke 9: 28–36.

The Legend of St Sergius and the Bear

Deep in the forest
birch and pine are creaking,
the wind playing its plaintive tune
in the moving canopy,
the light dappling and dancing
among berries and mushrooms
hiding on its floor.
And a lonely man
accustomed to long silences
sits outside his hermitage—
really no more than a small wooden hut—
wondering where the next meal
will come from.
One slice of bread remains,
the trencher he has used
as a plate these solitary days,
and it is stale and hard now, brittle.
Lost in his reverie
the man at first doesn't notice the approach
of a hungry bear
who boldly reaches out
for that last piece of bread.
It is all the saint possesses now—
can he give it up?
The wind in the trees sings
'Abide in me and you will never hunger,
give as I give even for the life of the world.'
There is no contest—
of course the bear must have this bread,
but as it swallows it
the muzzle reaches out again,
gently tugging at the saint's sleeve.
And together man and bear begin to dance
among the dappled bushes,

uncovering all the hidden fruits
the plants have been sheltering—
berries and mushrooms,
nuts, herbs, and nourishment
for every season
so that for many years
the saint will live here in his hut
in the friendly forest,
abiding in the love of Christ
and letting that love
abide and grow in him.

The story behind a wall painting at the Trinity Monastery, Sergiev Posad, Russia. Cf. John 15: 4.

Lazarite

Epstein's Lazarus looks displeased
to be back among the living,
as if in those few days since they put him in the tomb
he had become accustomed and almost adjusted
to death. Jesus' snort of passion
may have come as a rude awakening,
a calling back over the long and lonely road
to a world he was not sorry to leave.
But it is not a backwards step,
not a return journey he is making.
Rather it is a branching out
into something new and pulsating
with the promise of what Jesus
will himself bring back from death.
For now he is committed,
not just involved, but committed,
and we know exactly the agonizing road
he will walk. Will we hear the snort
and come out of our own tombs to follow him,
or will it seem too much effort, too dangerous, too hard?
Jesus was deeply moved by the death of his friend Lazarus,
so moved that he turned passion into Passion
for all our sakes. Let us emerge, then,
from our gloomy graves,
our sorry sepulchres,
and salute him with the winding-cloths
he commands them to untie.

The raising of Lazarus (partly inspired by Epstein's sculpture).
See John 11: 1–44.

Conveyancing

The invitation is to a new home,
a renewed body,
and a rising, rising up
out of the harrowing of hell.
The door to this new house
will open
in its own time,
in God's own time,
and it's no good
trying to short-circuit the process.
The train that takes us there
stops at every station,
all those crowded platforms
of shouting people
at first waving palms
but later their fists.
And the last stop, on Friday,
is deserted.
It comes in the night-time
of the day-time,
when the curtain is torn in two
and there seems to be
no protection, just abandonment.
All will seem lost
as God pays the price of love,
but in that very moment
we have redemption,
we have completion,
and something is conveyed
that the world has never seen before.
The key to the new life
is forged from iron nails,
placed in the lock by the one they mock,

and turned three times.
After that, no more looking
through the keyhole,
for the invitation is to a new body,
a new life—
come in, and make yourself at home.

Holy Week and Easter. See the ends of all four Gospels.

Hosanna Time

The bedside light reflected in the TV screen
is hourglass-shaped
and as we enter Holy Week
the sands of time are shifting once again,
filtering unavoidably
into the lower portion,
towards the quicksand
that will suck Christ in.
But today the top half is still full,
replete with praises
as a humble ass
makes its way into Jerusalem,
its footsteps quiet upon the quaking earth
carpeted with palms,
and on its back
the King of Glory riding.
It is the hour of the Hosannas
and it won't last long.
Make the most of it, Messiah,
before they turn on you
with weasel words and curses.
Time is running out
grain by grain into eternity
and the hourglass itself
will shatter. But you,
although they do their best to break you,
you will establish a new time,
time after instead of time before,
and everything, everyone
broken on the wheel of time
will be raised to the new era, mended.
And so Hosanna I will shout
with the best of them,
knowing I also may be found

among the worst of them,
but that your sacrifice
will save me just the same.

Palm Sunday. See Matthew 21: 1–9, Mark 11: 1–10, Luke 19: 28–38, John 12: 12–15.

Nil Carborundum

Monday of Holy Week,
the beginning of the end.
Or is it the end of the beginning?
I'm not quite sure.
Anyway, Jesus is surrounded
by the milling crowds
and watched by the wary leaders
who would trap him and catch him out.
They want him on the millstone,
imprisoned by his own teaching,
they want to grind him down,
grind him to harmless dust.
'Should we pay taxes to Caesar?'
they got somebody to ask,
and his reply was so simple
and yet so profound
that some of us have spent our lives
trying to divine its meaning.
Everything we have is God's,
so to render that back to God
is to give our whole lives
in reflecting the royal gift.
We are called to a life
of sharing what we have received,
but in the 'real' world,
the world of money matters,
the world *where* money matters,
but you must never let the bankers
grind you down.
Curiously, talk of coins
interrupted my prayer this morning
and the millstone has started grinding
deep within me.
Christ, let me see your face

on the coinage I transact today,
Jesus, let me see your face
in the people with whom I deal,
so that your love
may not be reduced to dust in me
but be invested in the world,
in the people you came to save.

The question about taxes. See Matthew 22: 15–22, Mark 12: 13–17, Luke 20: 19–26.

New Word

How many words are in the English language?
This is a question I've been asked many times.
And there is no simple answer
because the language is always growing,
recombining roots and affixes
and spitting out new combinations of letters.
I was going to make a new one this morning—
something never heard before,
something exciting and joyful.
But then I glimpsed it taking off
with a flash of turquoise and yellow,
a bird half hidden behind the screen of Holy Week.
And I realized I had been beaten to it.
For what word could be more exciting and joyful,
what word could convey greater meaning
than the Word of God rising from the ashes,
God's whole purpose resurrected for our sakes?

Anticipating Easter. See John 1: 1, 14.

Maundy Mantra

Bitter herbs are a sharp reminder of today
as Passover eve comes again to memory.
In cool blues and greys Christ gathers his friends around
him,
soon to fall silent, but not before
the long farewell is spoken
and love acts out its own humility.
This is my body, this is my blood:
such shocking words
and so hard for the disciples to understand.
But we have hindsight,
we have two millennia of tradition,
and there is no excuse for us to mistake their import.
Broken for you, shed for you: this mantra
maun mix itself into our very veins
as the red runs slowly out of the picture
and seeps on to that other canvas of the crucifixion.
Bitter herbs serve to remind us
that Christ gave himself to be the slaughtered lamb,
but first they heralded the great deliverance:
and now, once for all, they maun mean the same.

Maundy Thursday: the Last Supper. See Matthew 26: 17–29, Mark 14: 12–25, Luke 22: 7–20, John 13, 1 Corinthians 11: 23–6.

The Foot-Washing

Jesus, like Peter
I find myself both clinging desperately to you
and with the other hand
almost pushing you away.
I am holding your compassionate face
to my right breast
where I cannot actually see it
and looking over your other shoulder,
my left hand in a stop sign
saying, 'I cannot take this,
your love is more than I can cope with.'
Yet I know I must let you wash me,
not just my feet, but hands and head as well—
the hand that clings so as to touch more gently,
the hand that pushes back so as to come to rest
in a YES to all you have to give me,
all you invite me to.
And the head, the muddled head
more than anything needs soap and water
so that I can see again where you are leading me.
The basin Peter's feet are in
seems to have green leaves instead of water,
and in this picture you are kneeling in a pool
of deep blue, gemstone lapis sky.
Everything is upside down—the earthy colours,
the browns and ochres, greys and umbers
are above the horizon
while white and blue, turquoise and a tiny bit of yellow
put heaven on the floor,
where the Holy One's abased.
And this is the sign, as if I needed it
that if I am to be your disciple
I must let you turn me inside out,

reverse my priorities, shake up all my values,
and wash my dirty feet before they send you out to die.

Jesus washes his disciples' feet (partly inspired by a painting by Sieger Köder). See John 13: 2–15.

Love's Exclamation

Oh! My love, my dear one
what have they done to you?
Lacerated and chastised,
your body blue,
you stumble up that dolorous hill
as if already nailed to the wood,
even your halo barbed and thornlike,
yet sparking the cosmos in the name of good.

Eh? My love, my dear one
what have *I* done, how have *I* lent
my weight to your burden,
my sin to your body bent?
So many small betrayals
have brought you here.
It wasn't just Judas, was it,
but the whole rolling sphere
of human evil, which you seem to push
up the hill like Sisyphus, but more humble,
and which threatens to roll back
and crush you every time you stumble.

Uh! My love, my dear one
I can hardly bear to look
on your blue and broken body,
on the goodness they, *we* mistook
for threat, and lashed out in fear.
But if I do not look I will not see
how love triumphs—Ah!—because of you, my dear.

Good Friday (a meditation partly inspired by a painting by Constantina Wood). See Matthew 27: 27 ff., Mark 15: 16 ff., Luke 23: 11 ff., John 18–19.

Kenosis

God was poured out into flesh
but that was not enough to do the trick.
He healed so many—
of leprosy, of blindness, of possession,
and stopped the flow of blood of a dozen years
by a timid, hesitant touching of his cloak
because it was made in faith.
But still it was not enough,
and he knew it from that day on the mountain top.
He tried, he tried to tell them
that there would be further bloodshed,
but they could not hear him.
and so he went alone, almost,
poured out sweat and tears in the garden,
and finally his whole heart upon the cross.
This bleeding, battered heart
haemorrhaging a forgiving love
such as the world has never known before or since.
This sacred heart—
surely, surely, this must be enough?

God's self-emptying love in Jesus. See John 1: 14.

Crossword

Weep not for me, mother,
although the world's weight
rests on my shoulders
along with your parting embrace,
the dark shadow of the cross
behind us now
and the box below waiting
to transport me to the tomb.
Weep not, for what is finished
is but the conception
of the great beginning,
a birth you never knew
you had laboured for,
and this pain tearing
your motherhood in two
will rend the curtains of eternity
and from the darkness
deliver captives drawn out
by the forceps, by the forcefield
of sacrificial love.
This Caesarean section
is the wonder-wound
that separates for ever
evil from good.
Weep not, for the grief is nearly over.
It is almost time to celebrate
the new life born eternal
over which death
shall never more exercise dominion.

Contemplating the icon 'Weep not for me, mother', an Orthodox equivalent of the Pietà. Cf. Luke 23: 28 and see Romans 6: 9.

Time-Lapse Garden

Time between death and resurrection
when the tomb stands silent,
cold stone, silent,
its secret sealed away,
and the soldiers before it,
guarding the garden, guarding the body.
In this time between
the silence is thick and palpable,
for God does not speak,
God is dead and buried,
and they wonder will God ever speak again.
The gardener goes about his business
quietly. He prunes, he tidies
with hushed hands,
treading softly
so as not to disturb the sleeping earth.
And he has no idea
that soon he will be redundant.
Will the grass grow now
without God to bless it?
Will the spring come anyway
as it always does?
Growth, or any hope of it
seems sealed away itself
behind that stone.
How could the great adventure have ended
in this hollow silence,
this atrophy of all their hopes?
That stone is cruel and unyielding,
final, somehow.
The earth waits but expects nothing.
In this hushed hiatus
hope itself has died.
But just as you cannot hear

a leaf appearing from the bud,
just as you cannot see
the earthworms at their work,
just as you cannot witness
the tarmac cracking and yielding to a mere bramble,
so already change is happening
behind the stone.
God is stirring, waking Christ
to plough the furrow, go down and harrow
hell, to rescue patriarchs and prophets
and to bring Adam and Eve
back into the garden.
And tomorrow we shall have a new gardener
as life breaks forth,
stronger than any stone.

Holy Saturday. See Matthew 27: 66.

Sunlight on Stone

Spring sun
falling on a stone,
revealing its brightness
more than it can
yet bring it warmth;
but it is sunlight
from an unclouded sky,
and even the stone
can show it and reflect it,
even the stone
begins to shine.

How many years
of human language
would you have to teach it
before this stone
would start to speak?
Yet it takes only sunlight
and a little silence,
it takes but a moment
to make it expressive:
even the stone
is taught to talk.

There was a stone
heavy and forbidding
barring the entrance
to the tomb in the garden
where he'd been laid to rest;
they feared
to have to move it,
but the light of glory
had already flung it wide:
even the stone
made way for life.

Am I a stone
that these things
fail to move me,
that my tears
don't flow for you
and for the others
you died and rose to save?
Teach me to reflect you,
to make your light my language,
and even this stone
shall shine, and speak, and live.

Who rolled away the stone? See Matthew 28: 2, Mark 16: 4, Luke 24: 2, John 20: 1.

Joanna

I am Joanna; my name means 'the Lord has been gracious',
and I bless the day he brought Jesus into my life.
I was so ill, so sad, and life was a dirge for me
until the day he healed me and changed everything.
Then my dismal dervish-dance of death
became a joyful leaping jig of life.
I had it all, you know—
my husband is the keeper of Herod's coffers—
I never wanted for a thing.
But things were not what I needed, and Jesus saw that.
Rich in things and poor in soul, that was me,
but Jesus said that I would be happy,
that all the poor in soul would be happy,
that we would have the Kingdom of Heaven.
Well, I know what he meant now,
but first we had to follow him to hell before we saw it.
It wasn't easy being a follower of Jesus when my husband
was so well-to-do;
people bitched and muttered, even though I tried to use my
wealth
to make sure his ragged band had everything they needed.
But when the real suffering came, we women were all one
in our sorrow.
Poor, poor Mary—how could any woman be put through a
greater trial?
To see your son humiliated, tortured, ripped apart like that
and left to die in agony!
I don't think I could have survived it.
It was bad enough for all of us who loved him from afar.
Those gentle hands that had healed so many,
lifted children on to his lap, and blessed the poor and
hungry,
shaking with pain, bleeding, and cramped into agonized
claws.

Those clear, searching eyes darkened, that handsome,
sensitive face brutalized by thorns,
that graceful body through which such strength and spirit
flowed
hacked, racked, and ruined on a cruel cross.
I couldn't bear it, can't bear to think of it now
except to tell you how he healed even all of that,
how his light and life triumphed even over all the darkness
and hate.
I don't know how we got through that Sabbath, really,
but, somehow, we went through the motions,
wondering whether life could ever be liveable again,
wondering whether it was all for nothing that he had healed
us.
It helped to have something to do,
so we gathered together the spices to anoint his body
and planned our trip to visit the tomb.
At last there was a glimmer of light on the horizon and all
of us were ready to leave,
groping our way through the morning mist, our feet getting
soaked by the dew.
Funny, really, that we'd had so long to plan
but hadn't thought of the biggest problem—
how were we going to roll away the stone?
I thought of that as we got near the cemetery
and I remembered how it had taken several strong men to
roll it into place.
I imagined the heaving and pulling we'd have to do,
a grim ballet in the dawn light, even for such a crowd of
women.
But as I peered through the mist I thought my eyes were
deceiving me—
I could see the dark, round hole in the rock, and the stone
tossed aside like a cartwheel, not the solid lump of rock I
knew it was.

Well, we tiptoed into the dark cave
and started falling over each other as we felt for the body.
My hands moved along the smooth rock,
and soon I found the shelf on which it should have lain.
But the shelf was flat and stony, like the walls,
except for a roll of linen at one end.
'He isn't here!' we all began to say at once
as we stumbled around in the darkness.
Suddenly, though, the place was dark no more.
It was as if lightning flashed round the cave,
more blinding still than the darkness we'd been in.
Two figures seemed to be the source of light,
but I was too afraid to look at them.
'Why are you here among the dead?' a voice boomed out,
'Why look in a tomb for someone who's alive?
Don't you remember he told you he would die and rise
again on the third day?'
I thought of all the stories he had told, and of the awful
secret he had shared
about the need to die in Jerusalem.
But yes, yes, there had been something else—that God
would raise him up, yes that was it!
And I thought of how he'd told us we'd be sad
but then our joy would chase away all tears.
Salome said 'I see, oh yes, I see!' and rushed out into the
rising sun
and suddenly we all were dancing there,
joining hands and dancing in a ring.
I knew then that life really was made new—
that other Salome I'd seen dance for the king,
that evil dance, based on what people want—
all that was dead, and what we had was . . .
LIFE!

The women at the tomb: see Luke 8: 3 and 24: 10.

Mary Magdalene

Jesus cast seven devils out of me,
devils of lust, power, greed, dark, hatred, anger, pride.
When they were still at work in me they made my body
twitch,
making me seem to dance, but not in a graceful way.
And I had danced a different dance, languid and louche,
alluring to sinful men who willed my flesh.
So when the others danced, danced by his empty grave
I really couldn't join them; not just then.
They seemed like silly girls, chasing a ghost.
Besides, my grief was still raw—deep within
I could still hear his groaning, feel his pain
and sense the throb of loneliness in my hollow heart.
Would I never see my Jesus again?
Had he really been taken from me—
even his poor, inert body that I'd longed to dress
with my bitter herbs and the sweet perfume of love?
It was just *too* cruel.
At least I'd thought I could kneel there and say goodbye.
At least I'd thought I could linger over the sad farewells.
But no—he was gone, and my every sinew screamed
'WHY? Why have you taken my Lord away from me?'
How could he be alive when I'd seen him hanged,
my gentle Lord, crucified by hate,
he who was love itself, broken apart
and wasted by the treachery of men?
I knew he'd died—hadn't I died too
within my heart, as I stood and watched, shattered by grief?
So why did those glittering angels in the cave
say we were looking for the living among the dead?
I wanted to scream 'Don't try to shield me, don't pretend—
I know he's dead, just let me grieve in peace!'
Hot tears blinded me. I ran outside
to find the others running round in circles,

mad with their dreams, laughing and crying all at once.
Finally they ran off to share their fantasies.
I found a quiet corner and sank down,
racked with sobs, in another world from them.
I don't know how long I stayed there. Time seemed to stop.
But presently I was aware of someone else
and I seemed to hear a tune I thought I knew.
It was a man. I thought he was the gardener
or an attendant there to tend the graves.
My hope leapt up again—maybe he'd know
where the frail treasure I had sought was laid.
'Why are you crying?' he asked, so tenderly
I couldn't stop the tears springing afresh.
I told him, but I just stared at the ground,
hardly daring to look, I was so ashamed.
That tune again. Where had I heard it before?
And then my name. 'Mary.' Tender. The voice of love.
No-one else said my name like that.
I was transported to the day of my healing—
I could almost see the devils rushing out of me.
'You'll dance again—dance to the tune of love,'
that's what he had said, I remembered now.
All the evil would be washed away, I'd be redeemed.
'Oh Lord, it's really you! Can it be true?'
I reached out, but he wouldn't let me cling.
'Why aren't you with the others, sharing the joy?'
his clear eyes seemed to say. And then he was gone.
Suddenly I'm tripping, running, skipping, yes *dancing* to
that tune.
Quick, quick, I must catch up with them.
I must tell the men—our Lord and Christ's . . .
ALIVE!

The women at the tomb. See Matthew 28: 1, Mark 16: 9, Luke 24: 10, John 20: 11–18.

Glory

In the cool, dark tomb a flame.
In the winter-girded heart a spring.
Falls the melted ice upon the dust
and there springs GLORY.
Do not try to touch.
Do not try to say too much.
GLORY ABOUNDS
whether you understand
or not.

The empty tomb. See Matthew 28: 1–7, Mark 16: 1–8, Luke 24: 1–8, John 20: 1–9, 17.

fools gladly

blossom on a tree
we all thought dead
though the cold wind
still keeps us captive indoors
out only in our mufflers
and this tree flowering
is oblivious and forward
a character some would say
defines a fool

light in a cave
we all thought sealed
permanently darkened
by the stone that blocked the entrance
and hushed reverentially
shell-shocked and fearful
in the face of death
but then blasted open for any
fool to see

life in a body
we all thought cold
but warming as it quickened
and the grave clothes
lying to one side
discarded and unneeded
except to give the signal
to grieving women the men
dismissed as fools

suffering gladly
for all us fools
and then the unexpected
making a nonsense of the wise
giving hysteric women

the better part
in sharing the news
a role for which I'm glad
to be your fool

The women at the tomb. See esp. Luke 24: 11.

Get a Life

The road to Emmaus is hot and dusty,
heavy with disappointment,
strewn with great boulders of misunderstanding.
You want to keep silent on the way
but like an irritating insect
the biting, buzzing shock of failure
will not leave you alone
and you have to share it with your companion.
Round and round it goes
even though you keep batting it away,
flying backwards and forwards
in the oppressive, pulsing air,
zooming back in with a whine
just when you thought you had swatted it.
Dusk comes and you haven't reached the village
but you know you must trudge on
and you try to keep each other's spirits up
somehow. Then the whine of the mosquito
starts to sound like another human voice,
it begins to soothe rather than annoy
and suddenly there is a third person with you.
Where did he appear from? The boulders and the desert
keep the secret. Where has he been
not to have heard what happened in Jerusalem?
This stranger needs to get a life, you think.
But the odd thing is, he seems to understand
things you thought inexplicable. Suddenly
you cannot bear to lose his company just yet,
and the gathering darkness seems less gloomy.
You invite him to eat with you
now the village is in sight
and, as he breaks the bread and says those words
again, you see you are the ones
who need to get a life.

He has it, even though he died,
he's risen, as he promised you he would.
He leaves you now, but not before the bug
has bitten you, and you know you have to run
all the way back to Jerusalem
to tell his friends good news.

The road to Emmaus. See Luke 24: 13–35.

Incredible Love

As Thomas sticks his finger
right into the wounded side
of his beloved Jesus
in all the paintings of this scene,
he finds the evidence he's seeking,
not just that his friend
has really suffered
but that he's come out
on the other side.
Suddenly all of it is real:
the fear, the gore, the wounds,
the loss of hope
(those were real already)
but also life that goes on
beyond death,
the love that bears it all
and can alone survive it,
real love, tougher
for the scars it carries.
But Thomas was a twin,
and with the raw reality—
the fear, the wounds, the loss—
came the twin promise
of life and love renewed
for Jesus and this his brother.
Today we pray to God
to show us doubters
that love *is* real,
even more real than death,
and only grows
the more it suffers—
in short, that love
and life are siblings

and all *we* have to do
is just believe it.

Looking at paintings of 'doubting Thomas'.
See John 20: 19–29.

Peter restored to sense

a wisp of smoke rising
from a charcoal fire
gave the first clue
that he was waiting there
waiting to redeem
all the burnt hope
all the spent promises
the brazier of betrayal

as the boat was carried
empty back to shore
the incense from the fire
reached our nostrils
and its crackling
was carried on the breeze
along with his voice calling
try on the other side

the net was then so heavy
we all thought it would break
and the struggle to haul it in
strained our unaccustomed muscles
before mine were first
frozen by the sea
then warmed back to softness
by his breakfast blaze

finally the taste of fish
and acceptance once again
the savour of my Saviour's words
drawing me back in
my love three times protested
coating my tongue
and the knowledge that his
is a strong net never like to break

from petrified my senses
melt me into his embrace
oh thank you Lord

The risen Jesus appears by the lake. See John 21.

Put On the Shoes of Peace

The horseshoe of the Apostles,
each different in the face
yet seated similarly round the table,
waits there, waits and wonders.
They are one, as you prayed for them to be,
and yet each has a need
of the promised Holy Spirit
that is specific, unique, known to you alone.
Each waits in a capsule
of his own failures, his own hopes,
and when the wind begins to blow
and fans the flames to forge this horseshoe
we know the Church sets out on its life's journey,
spreading the message far and wide.
And yet for each spark to fly from the horseshoe at the
forge
there had to be one person, an individual
who said 'Send me.'
There had to be a spirit open to renewal,
a tongue supple to the supply of languages,
a vessel ready to be filled with wisdom,
a body physically prepared to make the journey.
And so you forged your horseshoe
but also refashioned the separate nails
to forgive this one who was weak from self-accusation,
free this other caught in the vicious circle
of darkness and misunderstanding,
heal the lameness in the resolve of a third,
stir up a fourth out of a confused stupor,
and so on through the whole body,
nails now straight and strong again so as to strike home
and hold the shoe in place on its long, long journey.
The horseshoe of the Apostles
in the Pentecostal icon

is upside-down according to the old wives' tale
of not letting the luck run out,
but to me it is all providence, all mystery
that the Spirit comes to each, even today
and forges something strong out of our weakness.
And so let me tell in whatever words are given
that God is merciful, the Comforter holds sway.

Pentecost (partly inspired by an icon). See Acts 2, Ephesians 6: 15.

The Ethiopian

What a long and dusty search it was,
a longing and a thirsting for those healing waters to engulf me.
Looking back it feels as though
my whole life had been spent on that weary journey.
Never quite accepted,
however successful I was,
however much money and power the Queen entrusted to me.
Even as a boy I was different,
set apart by the role that had been chosen for me,
set apart even more by the ritual I had to undergo.
The adults seemed to think it was a privilege,
but children can be cruel
and in my heart I believed their taunts.
There was something missing from my life,
and it wasn't just the physical and obvious.
I remember searching and seeking,
seeking something that would give my life meaning.
I started with my own people,
asking questions,
sometimes getting into trouble for it,
but when they couldn't help
I'd pester all the foreigners that came.
There must be some purpose,
some point to the world;
surely someone must know where it could be found.
The Jews I met seemed to have something,
a belief in the one God
who had made the world and everything in it,
who surely knew what its purpose was meant to be,
and who had chosen them for his own people.
Although their God got angry with them
he loved them like a parent

and couldn't withhold his love for long.
The more I found out
the more I wanted to know—
maybe this God could offer me
purpose and belonging.
And so I started to study
and to try to worship this God.
He had a holy city, Jerusalem,
and soon I realized I had to go there and see it for myself.
As I said, it was a long journey,
all the way through Egypt on a dry and dusty road.
We were hot and thirsty
and I ached from jolting about in the chariot.
I thought we'd never get there
but at last we saw the holy city in front of us,
and the Temple raised up in the centre of it.
My elation didn't last long, though,
because they wouldn't let me enter the Temple.
It was just another story of being excluded,
kept out because of my mutilation.
I felt bitter and defeated,
but somehow I couldn't believe
the God I had been learning to love
would really reject me.
Somehow I knew
that if I sought him in my heart
the rejection could be healed.
And at least I managed to buy a scroll of the Jewish scriptures,
pricey, but worth its weight in gold
if only it brought me nearer to belonging.
As we swayed along the dusty road home again
I tried to read it,
but although I could read the words
I couldn't get their meanings to hang together.
I found beautiful poetry in the writings of their prophets,

and I longed to understand them, to be refreshed by them
as I longed also to stop and rest
and drink my fill of cool, sweet water.
It was just then that I noticed another traveller on the road.
He was running, trying to catch up with us,
in that heat, too.
When he finally got his breath back
he asked me what I was reading,
and whether I understood it. And then,
when I said I didn't really understand
what the prophet said about God's servant
who suffered in silence and died in shame,
an amazing thing happened—
the man climbed up beside me, really close,
and started to tell me about Jesus.
Not only did this man accept and befriend me,
but he had come to tell me that God himself accepts me,
that I needn't suffer all my life on the outside,
despised and different,
because God's son, Jesus,
had won me a new life by dying on a cross
and rising from the dead.
Not only that, but all the dust and grime
of my old life could be washed away
and I could know myself clean, and loved, and free
by being baptized in Jesus' name.
Just then, as I looked up
I saw a pool of water shimmer in this wilderness
and everything around seemed to invite me to bathe.
I practically leapt into the water
to receive that healing baptism,
and I haven't looked back since.
As I came up out of the water
it was as if the prophet's words were coming true
in my life—water had appeared in the desert
and all the arid places seemed to be shouting for joy.

I know I was. One small sadness was
that I didn't get to thank the young man who baptized
me—
he disappeared as quickly as he had come.
But somehow I knew
that sharing his good news with other people
and washing them clean as well in baptism
would be more than thanks enough.
And I haven't found that difficult—
it's as though a fountain sprang up within me that day.
It bubbles and it flows with the love of Jesus,
the Messiah;
he lives within me, and I in him,
fertile and fruitful finally
on his vine,
in the garden only God could nurture.

Philip baptizes a Gentile seeker. See Acts 8: 26–40.

The Gardener Speaks

Be still, my child, and do not fret.
Be still, and stop your frantic struggling.
You only need to seek me in your heart,
incline the ear of your heart,
open the eyes of your heart,
and you will know me with you once again.
Turn to me,
gaze on me
and see how much I love you.
Do you think I'd ever give you up?
Turn to me,
gaze on me,
try to turn away from all your failings.
Don't you think I know you through and through?
Turn to me,
gaze on me,
leave me to decide how best to show you
that you
your struggles
all the world's pain
are for me to gaze on.
You can look at me and find great beauty:
when I gaze on you I find the same.
Be still, my child, and do not fret.
I am with you, always.

The final assurance. See Matthew 28: 20, Revelation 21: 3–4.

III

For the World

Praying and Sharing

One World

He held it in the palm of his hand,
a little jewel,
glowing green and aquamarine,
sparkling with life and beauty.
Compared with his greatness
it was a tiny thing,
this jewel,
no more than a marble
thrown into the sky.
Yet every speck of colour
opened a gate of glory,
his glory
spread out on the land.
It held his power,
awful and wonderful,
mysterious and dangerous,
contained in the throbbing ball.
There were many worlds
within it,
worlds of plants and fishes,
people, animals, birds.
Each world itself was many,
millions of each species,
no two made the same.
Yet at its heart
was a silver secret
holding it all together,
making it truly one.
Love was its unity—
one Word, one world.
Love made it precious.
A tear fell on his jewel—
would they *ever* understand?

Verdant

Everyone needs a green space to look at—
this is the policy I heard the other day.
In the inner city
rather than knives and gangs
a flash of emerald
would strike home to the heart,
stabbing it with beauty
and replacing rivalry and violence.
A glimpse of blossom pink or white
would offer a new skin
to the bruised and lonely,
a single flower opening
might be enough
to overcome the closure of hope.
But not only there
are excellent and lovely vistas needed—
wherever there is the jungle,
be it concrete or metaphorical,
the invitation to the garden
must be spoken
graciously, lovingly,
and on the Gardener's behalf.
And the green hill far away
of which we used to sing at primary school
would be brought close,
as close to us as breathing.

Lingua Franca

There are ways of speaking
that use no words,
their phrasing sketched
by minute lines
appearing and disappearing
round the eyes
or by the ballet of a hand
coming to rest just so
after shrugging the air.

There are ways of signalling
that something must be said
for which the words
can't be found yet,
but will appear
in the waiting space
between two people
who sit expectantly in silence,
trusting each other.

No dictionaries exist
to list the lexicon
of this language of the spirit,
no grammars from which
you can study its syntax.
Rather you must learn it
by being there,
by total immersion
in the situations

for which it is the mother tongue,
attuning your ears
to its quiet cadences,
acquiring the deep structure
of a look, a gesture, or a touch

and waiting,
patiently waiting
for the right time
to speak.

Freshwater Pearl

A raindrop on the windowpane,
its essence held
only by the surface tension
as it hesitates
not quite ripe to flow,
the shimmering meniscus
almost invisible
except as the strength
still holding it together
until the moment
of its full expression,
storing its meaning,
hugging its wetness
into a transparent pearl.

A teardrop filling
from an eye,
squeezed out
between the rows of lashes
and bulging
as surface tension
holds its potential roundly
in its grasp;
the pearl this time of passion
and the meniscus memory,
the drop fat with feelings,
and the moment of expression
when finally it comes
is a release.

To hold this tension safely
and gently feel
the moment when the meaning
is ripe to flow,
to honour another's passion,

letting memories
leave their meniscus,
yet still recognize
that the surface tension
was their strength—
this is communication,
a two-way trust
translating the ineffable
into flowing grace.

Sword of Truth

Light is not the absence of the dark
but the sight in shadowed places
of its complementary colour
hope opalescent
by its own deep concentration
silvering the storm clouds
into brightness.

Love is not the opposite of hate
but the kindling of pure passion
out of which may follow
the silencing of all recrimination
all competition
as in the presence of the beloved
comes forgiveness.

Peace is not the absence of a war
but the spreading of Shalom
that overflows the spirit
with acceptance
diluting all our differences
so that any conflict
becomes pointless.

Truth is not the opposite of lies
but a bold bright blade
raised as a beacon before us
straight sword
cutting through all falsehood
so that hope, love, peace can blaze forth
into life.

Displacement

We buy so many books on prayer
hoping the next might hold the secret
but then don't even get around to reading them
thinking their combined weight
must count for something in the tonnage
of our spiritual street cred.
Yet all they really do is clutter up the shelves
and fill the internal spaces
where silence might have got a look-in
and prayer have become an open secret
free of all words, all time, all physical constraints.
This mysterious vessel sails by simple breath
the tide of awareness moving in and out
on the sea of our deepest longings
its hold appearing empty at first glance
but displacing all our heaviness
with transparent tomes of love.

Fear

Where does fear reside?
In the brain, where its warnings
are formed into words?
In the stomach, where it takes on wings?
In the heart, where it clamps the chest in panic
and at the same time palpitates the blood?
Or is it further down?
The fear that reaches furthest cramps the guts
and boils the bowels into liquid lava,
brands you with shame like a red-hot poker,
followed by steel and ice.
Is fear a speech bubble, an insect, or an infarction,
a volcanic eruption, a branding iron, or a cold knife?
Or is it just anything the imagination
can make the body suffer?
If so, its tyranny can be broken by imaging relief.

This is an experiment worth the making:
to speak peace to fraught thoughts,
eat a digestive biscuit of the soul,
breathe deep relaxation instead of panicked gulps,
take it so far in that even the blood flows slower,
let the smooth muscle spread and the knots dissolve,
and then rest in the sacred sacral chamber
where you are really you.
Take each new breath down through these levels like a
benison,
stepping back only if your focus fails;
but if you must step back, do it lightly,
the better to advance again with calm.
The in-breath carries composure, convects compassion,
sees all things, accepts all things, and transforms them;
then the out-breath lets the fear escape,
for once it is outside you it is robbed of power.

Abide here, then, and know who you are:
a person free of shame, imperfect but understood;
a person who is grounded in the present moment;
a person who has nothing left to fear.

Our Poem I

Out of three colours
and a clutch of notes,
out of a single Word
you make each of us
into a concerto,
into a picture
needing both dark and light.
On this great canvas
is our hate and love,
our restlessness and peace,
and all of it
held firm in an embrace.
Faced with this excellence
what can we humans do?
Well, nothing, really,
except perhaps to trust
and love all that you love
in thankfulness and joy.
The wine of our contentment
is that you hold us all
like crushed grapes
but skin and pips as well.
For where is our wholeness
without shadow,
and where is our harmony
without dissonance?
All of it is held in your hand,
the hand that broke the bread
and offered up the wine.
We shall not do,
but BE
in quiet thanksgiving,
and sing with all creation: Alleluia! Amen.

Our Poem II

In unexpected sunshine
and the blue perspective
of sea and sky
there was fun and friendship,
fellowship and more fellowship,
mixed with the rest
and relaxation
of a holiday.

But it went further too:
seeds were sown for our improving.
Learning to centre-down
into a rest so profound,
revealing the surprises of being,
reflection led to wholeness,
a new perspective,
reassurance, encouragement, and faith.

Not just relaxing on the beach
do you encounter
the bare midriff,
but waiting in the silence
for that other meeting
with the one
who alone fulfils
our deepest yearning.

Out-Breath

Instead of the daily drivel
recording but the minutiae of feelings,
I want to write about the important stuff.
Yet it seems the muse is too drugged, or asleep,
and so I simply hold the situation
trustingly up into your beam of love.
Even this I know is a small concern
and maybe too petty therefore to attract you
busy as you are with so much greater things.
But I do believe that great stream flows between you,
the eternal prayer of Christ to a loving Father,
and that the Spirit moves to keep it flowing.
And even if I cannot find the words,
that same Spirit fans the message onwards
and joins it to the breeze that freshens things.
Let me be content, then, with a breath,
a sigh even, but one lifted to a thermal.
Let me be content to be a feather
and all of us to float gently on this current.
We know not where it blows, but we will trust it,
knowing it is the breath that makes all one.

Respect

Those boys in the TV programme
caught up in gangs and a senseless life of crime,
in rising violence, searching in the wrong corner
for something called 'respect'—
they haunt me.
It was a fiction, but founded on the facts,
the cruel facts of life
in too many of our cities and estates
and the hardest fact not life,
but death.
When young lives are so cheap
and the culture of keeping silent
makes them worth less every day
as no-one ever pays the price of crime,
what does 'respect' amount to?
Its value plummets like the financial markets
and is distorted more than the exchange rate.
O God, give us a new currency
with which to measure all humanity—
we say you paid the price of sin,
exchanging our bad debts for eternal life:
take pity on these empty lives,
take pity on our humanity so narrowed,
teach us the respect with which
you gently touched and healed lives we'd devalued.
Lord, have mercy, have mercy on our souls.

Were You There, Immanuel? Are You Really God-with-Us?

(reflecting on an icon of Immanuel in the light of reports of child abuse)

Immanuel, teenager in a Superman cape,
looking out at me from the heavenly blue,
you had the wisdom to confound the teachers of the Law.
Yet you are not Superman—
you don't fly to the rescue of every damsel in distress
and you couldn't save all those children from abuse.
Why do you not intervene before the damage is done?
Why do you not stop the monsters in their tracks?
It is hard, very hard to take
that so many fragile, vulnerable lives are ruined
and still you don't step in to rescue them.
These children grow up into frightened adults,
damaged and unable to find love in their lives—
or, sometimes worse, perpetuate the abuse,
adding sin to sin, hurt to hurt, tragedy to tragedy.
What have you to say to today's teachers of the Law,
what to the children and teenagers of our world?
To the teachers, can you give some words of wisdom?
To the youngsters, can you give direction and comfort?
You were a human child once, and you elevated children
to the heirs of the Kingdom, the first to enter heaven.
Your halo is yellow, but you surely aren't chicken;
you stood up to the bullies even as a child.
So say to the adults: Stop and consider,
respect and protect my little ones.
And to the children: I am with you, even when you cannot
know it.

Were You There, Immanuel? Are You Really God-with-Us? Revisited

(on the day for remembering the Massacre of the Innocents, just after a mass shooting of children at a school in Connecticut)

It's a day I still remember well,
All the news of abuse, and the fuss,
And I railed 'Were you there, Immanuel,
Are you really God-with-us?'
I saw you in your Superman cape,
For you were just a child, too;
And I wanted to see how you'd make them flee
As you donned this costume from under the tree;
Now we're back to the day when they have their way,
The wretches—so where are you?

You were there asleep in the oxen stall
That night when the angel came;
O, Bethlehem's babies were all so small
And all so free from blame!
Good Joseph got you away from there
Before Herod's henchmen came through;
But as Sandy Hook weeps, do the angels keep
A vigil for twenty more babes asleep?
For I have to say that they've had their way,
The wretches—and where were you?

Herod's anger made you a refugee
And in Egypt you lived for a while;
Then the old king died, and you were free
To return from enforced exile.
You grew up in a carpenter's shop
And maybe you worked there, too;
All that Scripture relates of your youth's the debate
With the Temple teachers that day you stayed late:
Mary cried, 'Lackaday, who has taken away
My child?', but at home there were you.

Much later you made your home on rough ground
With the outcast and damaged and lame,
As you travelled the road, you gathered them round
And fed them and gave them a name.
You said that a cup of water for these
Was sweet slaking for God's thirst, too;
You healed and you taught, told stories that brought
Justice to those the high-ups made naught,
Which hastened the day when they had their way,
And hung on the tree were you.

So now as we end this Christmastide
And dismantle the crib and the tree,
I'll remember the places where you still abide
With the mournful and refugee;
It was for *all* wretches you spilled your blood,
And by grace we can all be made new;
You forgave the good thief, and offer relief
To anyone struggling with darkness or grief;
So lullay, happy day that your love holds sway,
God-with-us, for right here are you!

Storm Child

It is a muggy morning
and energy is crackling in the atmosphere,
creating a rumbling line of thunderstorms
threatening from the west.
The storm is coming
and hatches need to be battened down
as the trees bend and sway in the wind.
For a young boy in London
the storm has already been and gone,
the blade tearing at his flesh
and leaving him the twelfth youth murdered
there this year alone.
For his family the storm will go on raging,
and also for the family of two- and six-year-olds
found dead from violence in a car.
Whole years have passed
since the disappearance of a little girl
whose family has been ravaged
by the incessant storm of media speculation
and by bewilderment and loss
crashing against the shores of Portugal.
All over the world
police continue to uncover
the evidence of cruelty and abuse
visited on innocent children.
The thunderstorms will pass
and we shall have warm weather,
the summer surely coming in
on the heels of spring.
But the lightning that has struck these lives
will leave them blackened, marred for ever,
and even the soft rains of summer
cannot wash away the hurt.
Thunder will always go on threatening

to break a new storm of grief
on the families left behind,
echoing with the memory
of children once bright with promise.
How can you let this happen,
God whose name is Love,
how can you let your little ones
be swallowed by the storm?
Can you not calm the wind and waves
as once you did in Galilee,
can you not control the lightning
you yourself have made?

'Peace, be still. I have already done it
when the sky turned black
and my own sweet child
was murdered on the tree.
I have already done it, don't you see?
For my Son is risen and ascended,
and my arms wait now to carry
every mourner who turns to me.'

Unreal

The thing you think you fear the most,
ironically, might turn out to be
something you long for secretly,
its payoff letting you escape reality.

Strange motives and even stranger wiles
of the distorted and distorting mind
can flood the body, clamp the breath, and bind
the will, till it can no longer find
any strength or courage to carry on.

Then what is needed is not to drive
harder, not to prosecute or force,
and certainly not in any way to endorse
your own harsh judgements,
but to hold the soul's remorse
in gentle hands, loving yourself back into reality.

Whatever You Ask For

Exhaustion dulls the gift,
interrupting its flow with apathy
and it is all that I can do
to make the pencil stay on the page.
Images arise but seem far off
behind a fog of sickening dreams
and the night's wrestling match,
which leaves me aching
as if kicked in the kidneys all night.

Reach out, reach up,
pull yourself into the day,
for this moment will not be repeated
and if you just turn over and curl up
you will extend the night
and make darkness your medium.
Open your eyes
to the promise all about you
and believe you are not alone
as you struggle towards the light.
Believe you have already received it
somewhere in the recesses of energy,
believe it is cloistered there
with your courage, waiting to be picked up.
Believe you have already received it
and it will be yours.

The Cry

The newborn baby fills its lungs and wails,
until which moment none can say
whether life has truly begun.
The need for air becomes addictive,
with gulping, hiccupping, and mewling time about
until the membranes, those minuscule balloons
hidden in the chestspoon,
open completely like parachutes,
allowing the soul to soar,
sucking the human spirit into every wingbeat.
How many million times is this small miracle
repeated in a life, but never marvelled at?
And then at the end there is a like delay,
breaths lagging three- or fivefold
behind the fleeing of the spirit,
breaths becoming slower, shallower,
until they are no more
and neither is the person yet dwelling behind the face,
but vanished on one of those breaths.
And even if you are there watching for it,
you cannot rightly say exactly when it happened,
only that it's gone.
And you can suck in air to your own chestspoon
to keen, to wail, to mourn the passing of one loved,
to send your cry as outrider for the beloved spirit,
but knowing it must turn back at the last
and return to you alone.
Perhaps you cannot do this straight away—
for years even—but the breathing miracle
continues gently underneath your grief
and one day you realize you are ready
to let out a cry, like the newborn child
helplessly bewailing the loss of the womb's cocoon,

of warm togetherness,
but also filling your lungs with the power
to return to your life.

WISDOM: Word, Image and Story, Doors of Mystery

Through word, image, and story
I approach the doors of mystery,
swinging open the chambers of the soul.
It is silent here, on the threshold of discovery,
the space beyond shadowy and brooding,
the Other waiting there as I wait,
catching my breath. Nothing moves
unless it is images rising into mind,
the connections being made with story
as shapes on the cave wall seem to suggest a presence.
Let the breath go fully, and with it all the fear,
let all hindrances leave the waiting body
until the chestspoon is ready to receive again,
filling naturally and calmly. Then step forward
knowing there will appear in the shadows
something made for your eyes alone,
a secret you must translate into poetry
so that others can see it too, and wonder.

Delayed Reaction

Living on automatic pilot
in a snowscape
that leaves the senses numb,
the whiteout helpful
in that it allows
long periods of coasting
over frozen feelings,
but treacherous too
as ice beneath the surface
sends the heart tumbling
unexpectedly
into an avalanche
of grief.

How do you put the colour
back into this monochrome?
How do you restore feeling
to the cold extremities
without unleashing
an explosion of throbbing pain?
How do you clear
the path of ice
without the salt that stings
in recent wounds,
without the grit
that grates against
the grain?

The thaw must be allowed
to come naturally,
in its own good time.
There is no sense
in forcing it,
for the waiting is itself

the core of healing.
Mind and body know
when spirit's tendrils will unfurl,
become an open hand,
and green be added
to the palette once again, reaching for
the spring.

Early Days

The recent past
is littered with memories
of struggle,
the present with arrangements
to be made,
and it's hard to get a clear view
into life lived joyfully.
Yet even in the struggle
there was laughter,
even in the admin
a sense of purpose,
and the shadows falling
give a roundedness,
a reality
to what might otherwise
seem flat and lifeless.
There is a different landscape now,
hazy perhaps,
not yet awoken
fully to its dawn;
and to walk there alone
without the reassurance
of that familiar hand
seems daunting,
scary even,
maybe impossible.
Help may be needed
to see the love that links
the journey remembered
with the one barely started on;
not alone but beckoned to,
invited
into a new companionship
living in mind and heart.

What

Maybe it is not the words
and not the absence of them either
not the sound
nor yet the silence.
Maybe it is not the image
and not the blank screen's blackness
not the familiar
nor yet the sight we miss.
Maybe it is not the thought
and not the clearing of the mind's wastes
not a memory
nor yet a wish unborn.
What is it that
you want to show us?
An empty husk
from which all life
has broken out
and the tiny kernel
of the emerging.

Transformations

I haven't used this staircase in a while
and it is dank and dusty,
its treads creaking as I make my way
down from the world of things and thoughts
into another atmosphere, to silence.
Here even the rule of time's suspended
and everything is naked—
no hiding behind the usual trappings.
It is not a threatening space, though,
this inner chamber always waiting
for me to enter and be laid bare,
since with the superficial outer clothing
it also strips me of the mind's accusations,
or at least lets me see them in another light.
Here I am accepted as I am
and each charge laid against me
can be considered calmly, in proportion,
given its own chance for growth and learning.
Here to say 'I'm sorry' is not abject prostration
but an opening for renewal to be realized.
Here to say 'I love you' does not attach
any weight of worldly obligations
but frees the spirit to be truly whole,
undiminished in its role of giving.
Here to be thankful even for the hard
is not 'bad times are just around the corner'
but seeing that in love *all* may be transformed—
all thoughts and feelings, but all people too.
And so I try to breathe these affirmations
out into the womb of my understanding
that they might be sown and born beyond me,
giving life wherever love is shared.

Word Order

The day of the Lord
is not at all the same thing
as the Lord's day,
one a day of judgement
for those of us—all—
who fall, who fail,
a day of retribution,
the other—one of celebration,
a weekly remembrance
that our faith is based on rising.
And so they seem to move
in opposite directions,
the day of the Lord downwards
with a chop,
surprising the wicked
like a thief in the night,
the Lord's day ever upwards,
lifting the faithful
with blessed regularity
like yeast working away silently
to raise the loaf.
But actually
there is only one direction
of love and justice shared—
for all of us are both sheep and goats
and even judgement
is a part of God's compassion
for the world.
God doesn't see in black and white
or why would there be colour?
Rather God can shed true light
to let us realize for ourselves
how much we need the shepherd,
to let us understand

how we've trampled the pastures
and stirred up the waters
until everything's as clear as mud
and paradise is spoiled for others,
to find it in our hearts to send
our goatish butting away into perdition
and turn like lost sheep to the one
who never gives up seeking us,
believing all need to be saved,
all can be saved,
all saved to the uttermost.
There is no condemnation, then,
except the light, the prophet's word
that teaches us to judge ourselves
as we really are—
but gives the strength to turn again
away from all self-loathing and despair.
So day of the Lord and Lord's day
can be the same—
the King triumphant,
and we? Rising, riding,
borne up by the glory of his name.

Engaged Spirituality

Yes, my beloved, you do engage with me—
you hold me with your love,
clutch me in a passionate embrace,
then release me into the world
with the memory of your touch
upon my face.
Free, then, yet still engaged—
still held in the promise
that binds me to you
and to others.
Today, being invited into the garden,
I retraced the steps that I travelled by your grace,
out of the darkness,
out of the necessary jungle,
and standing at the crossroads
between death and life.
And I remembered the others
who sat beside me in disordered worlds,
whose darkness touched me
as mine also touched theirs.
How we communed in silence
and together touched the mystery
that despair and chaos shared
can lead to life.
And I remembered, too,
the ones who didn't make it.
My dear Irina,
how I watched her sleeping,
never knowing that so soon
she would enter the sleep that never ends.
And if I make a pilgrimage
it will be to her home town of Iași,
to ask forgiveness for all those letters
I never wrote.

Connection is so important,
like those calls across the miles,
engaged with Joan.
When I saw your hand
reaching out in the jungle,
inviting me into the garden,
I thought I would only be joined with you.
But you were calling me to a marriage,
to an engagement
with growth in all its forms,
to place your ring upon the hands
of all I meet.

Passion Fruit

There is a difference,
such a substantial contrast
between standing with strength of spirit
and the pushing forward
of the ego.
To allow one's spirit to rise up
against the raging of the world,
to let it stand there, being ravaged
and yet becoming stronger for it—
that is passion,
it is the suffering that Christ turned into victory,
it is the essence of the Covenant Prayer.
'Put me to doing, put me to suffering,' we pray,
and by that we don't mean that we ask for pain
(although often pain will be involved),
but that we resolve to stand as steady as the cross
and take the nonsense that the world
is throwing at us without flinching
and without letting it diminish
by one iota, one jot or tittle
the love that roots the cross so deep,
the strength that quarters us,
making us both cruciform and grounded,
both foursquare to the world and domiciled in heaven.
To stand on these foundations
is not to push forth the ego,
which would seek comfort and revenge
always over sacrifice.
It is, quite simply, passion
and, although the fruit appears battered
on the outside,
its succulence and beauty
are at once revealed
if you but cut it open.

Adventure

November has almost run its course
and we step out into the great Adventure,
peering through the murk and mist
for the tender compassion of our God.
Dawn will surely come to us,
rising above our blind consumerism
and showing us the path of peace—
but will we let our feet be led there?
For this to happen, awe and mystery
must become our daily exploration,
opening new windows on the mind of God—
surprising, shocking even in their bias to the poor
and certainly not cosy images, not self-satisfied.
Show us the wider picture, Lord, the panorama
that sheds light into our darkest places
and give us the courage to act on what we see
so the Word may speak flesh into full humanity.

Lent

It is a dual journey, this season,
but in both directions it brings you home.
In both directions it leads to the cross,
and home is there, where the Son rises.
First, you must break the dry husk
and find the tender seed on the point of dying,
examine the rotten wood at the core of your being
and lift it gently to expose the creatures
that have made their home there.
Yes, they are creepy-crawlies, and maybe you recoil,
but they are living proof that even what is rotten can be
used.
Even what you thought lost can be redeemed.
Now, take this knowledge as your armour-plating
and like a slater persevere in that other journey
be it oh so slow,
the journey outwards
across the vast wastes and the open spaces,
across the deserts and the jungles
to the jumbled townscapes where people make their
dwelling.
If you are tempted to give up,
if it seems too far or your courage falters,
think of that slater you saw on the wide plains
of the front-room carpet,
journeying on across all that emptiness.
Have you not got a higher purpose?
Did Christ not set you free to share good news?
Slaters are prehistoric creatures, so I'm told.
Maybe they even colonized the cross.
I don't know that.
But I am coming home, to watch the sunrise.

One Day Lily

One day a flame will burn
in the hearts of the multitude
and all will glimpse the glory
God has wanted us to see.

One day the orange tongues
of the Spirit will be dancing here
and all will hear the language
that declares us healed and free.

One day we all shall meet
in the land we have called paradise
and realize it's the garden
of our shared humanity.

One day the peace-flower will bloom.

Unreasonable?

The way the light is falling on the ivy
I seem to see a boxer dog
asking me to play
from the top of the sycamore.
But I have just heard the view expressed
that the companionship of dogs
(put in the same bracket as belief in God)
is essentially unreasonable
and a matter of opinion
coming from within ourselves.
Why does this word *opinion*
keep cropping up at the moment,
tied inextricably with the word *unreasonable*?
The same speaker used them
of art, literature, and culture—
for him, it seems, only money
is either reasonable or real.
What a poverty-stricken picture
of humanity he has,
what a barren wasteland
his inner landscape must be.
Of course, in a sense,
all our beliefs and blessings
are unreasonable,
because we get so very much more
than we reasonably deserve;
and with the limited reason
we have been born with
it is hard to grasp the length, breadth, height,
and depth of God's love for us.
But this is where companionship
from a dumb animal
who is always pleased to see us
and holds nothing at all against us

can expand our minds.
This is where cold reason
becomes irrelevant,
not, as the speaker said,
proving the irrelevance of God,
but quite the opposite:
God's the one who's unreasonable
to love us unconditionally—
but, as John Taylor pointed out,
it's really quite ridiculous of God,
but in the end what can you do?
That's just the way God chooses it to be.

Blessings

Prayer cannot earn them,
nor can we assume
that just because we pray
they will be showered upon
those we would see blessed,
whether ourselves or others.

The prayer that simply cries
'Oh, please!', or even cannot find
any words, nor a sigh or groan
for the Spirit to alight on
and translate, that prayer
is just as lucid before God
as the practised excursion
into flowery language
from the lips of a priest.

Maybe more so for its sincerity,
for taking the risk of believing
there's anything out there
to appeal to, for exposing
the soft underbelly of need
where it is most vulnerable
and letting it be touched,
as if licked clean by a beloved dog.

In French *blesser* is to wound,
and it is the strange currency
of prayer that our readiness
to reveal our wounds
can be repaid to us in blessings,
in the touch of compassion upon us
or simply in the crying out itself
echoing back an answer
from the vibrating air.

And still we cannot earn it
or deserve it, and yet
by some mysterious conversion
our desperate 'Oh, please!'
affords us the strength to carry on,
for in the very act of praying
there is almsgiving, and the alms
are given to us and not by us,
and those alms are blessings.

Biblical Index to Section II

Typeset in Scala and Scala Sans
by George Tulloch